AMONG

THE

GRAVESTONES

AMONG THE GRAVESTONES

AMONG THE GRAVESTONES

A RECOLLECTION OF MY CHILDHOOD

BY

TOM LAIRD

AMONG THE GRAVESTONES

Copyright © 2023 Tom Laird

All rights reserved.

ISBN: 9798395672230

Cover Design

Tom Laird

CONTENT

9 INTRODUCTION

17 THE LIGHT THROUGH THE PINK

25 THE OLD BUILDING

33 THE GRAVEY

40 THE MUCK

45 THE CASTLES

48 THE SUGAROLLY MTS.

50 THE QUARRIES

54 THE STORY

59 THE SKI JUMP

64 COWBOYS AND INDIANS

70 THE BLUEBELL WOODS

75 MARBLES AND CONKERS

78 THE PRIEST

81 ST. PAUL'S PRIMARY

88 THE SEASIDE

AMONG THE GRAVESTONES

CONTENT CONT.

91 FIRST COMMUNION

93 CINNAMON STICK

96 TOAD IN THE HOLE

100 THE WINTER

103 RADIO AMD TELEVISION

108 NEW HEIGHTS

111 SHETTLESTON BATHS

116 THE BOWERY

121 THE PICTURES

125 BUTCHER'S BOY

133 LONG TROUSER SUIT

139 MY PALS

149 ON REFLECTION

AMONG THE GRAVESTONES

INTRODUCTION

When I went back to Shettleston to take some photographs for the book. I was standing at the corner of Killin St. taking a photo of the Kirkhouse building, a man passed by and was stopped by an acquaintance who appeared from behind me. He looked over at me and must have been wondering who the nosy old bugger was.

I thought I'd explain by saying "I was taking a photo of the house that I used live in". "Oh, when was that?" he asked. "Back in 50's until the late 60's, but my mother stayed there until the mid-80's," I replied. "But I was brought up in the old building that used stand where the pub car park is now" I said.

He went on to say, "The building is empty now, I thought you were thinking of buying a house", what's your name?" he said. "Laird, Tom Laird", I replied. "I was just curious, my name is Gerry Cavelle, I've worked in the Railway Tavern for forty-one years, since 1981, and I'm considered to be the google of the pub, anything the customers want to know, they come and ask me".

"Anything they want to know about the history of the place. There used be an old couple who stayed in the top left hand flat, they would phone us if they ever saw young boys on the roof of the pub after closing time". " That would be Mr. and Mrs Smillie", I said. "So the photo is just for your memories" he said. "No I am writing a book about my childhood, and this is me adding some photos," I hastily replied.

"If you had more time I'd tell you my story as you're the google of the pub". " Well why don't you come in for a coffee and tell me", he replied. "Are you sure you've got time?" I asked. "No problem, this is my day off, I can't stay away from the place, it's in my blood," he quipped with a wry smile.

WELL GERRY, IT SORT OF GOES LIKE THIS............

AMONG THE GRAVESTONES

TOM LAIRD

MY FAMILY

Da and Ma
Sadie and Ellen

AMONG THE GRAVESTONES

My sister Ellen, Ma, Da, and myself

AMONG THE GRAVESTONES

THE LIGHT THROUGH THE PINK

I've often said to my wife, that I seem to have memories of hearing muffled sounds and moving shadows, through an orangy/pink hazy light, which I seem to think, that I had a vision of what it was like being in my mother's womb. You may think this is crazy, but seemingly an unborn foetus at various stages of its development, can be aware of sound and movement outside the womb.

I was beginning to doubt myself and pursued the question. In my quest I found there is a woman whose name is Rebecca Sharrock, who has these memories and not only that, but she can remember every single day of her life which she is in the process of writing a book about.

Anyway apart from the womb my memories are pretty good but sketchy, and I will endeavour to recall them. I was born in Stobhill Hospital 5th November 1949. (Guy Fawkes night). I weighed in at 6lb 4oz and my mother said I was born at 6.00am, but my birth certificate states a different time.

At the time my family lived at Kennedy St. Townhead Glasgow. I have two sisters, Sadie and Ellen nine years and eight years older than me. Sadly Sadie passed away. I didn't know the size of the Townhead house, but after finding out from my sister Ellen it was a single end. about two weeks after I was born the family moved to Shettleston in the east end of Glasgow.

The house was a single end in an old building opposite to the old part of the Kirkhouse Inn. Opening the main door to enter the house into a stone porch and then opening the living room door on the left-hand side. Facing you were two bed recesses, one of which I would share with my Ma and Da, the other recess my sisters would sleep in.

The floor was covered with a floral-patterned linoleum, covered in the centre with an Axminister rug, where sat a drop leaf extendable table. Above this hung a circular glass light shade that hung from the ceiling by the means of three chains. Apart from providing light for the single end, it acted as an efficient fly catcher.

To the left was the adjoining wall to the house next door. Here stood the fireplace. It was made of cast iron, with a high mantel piece, where my Da would keep his clocks. ("Noaks", he'd call them, I think he made that word up). He would keep them at two different times, one at the right time and the alarmed one fast. The reason behind that was that he didn't want to be late for his work. Below at the grate stood a companion set, that housed his favourite poker.

The window wall you could look out on to the stepped gable of the old Kirkhouse Inn that they were now using as storage for the new Kirkhouse pub that was on the corner of the building at Shettleston Rd. Next to the old inn was Hassard the coalman's yard that used to be stables where he kept two lorries, as well as renting out some small garages.

Turning full circle, this led to the lobby door which was at the end of the window wall. The lobby was no more than approx. 5ft*5ft, that housed the coal bunker in the porch which was the entrance and exit to oor wee house. If I remember right, the building housed about eighteen families. I can remember some of their names. These were McMahon, McAloon, Travers, Deery, Wilson, Lindsay, and Dempsey whose son was my pal Tommy.

At the backend of the building stood two air raid shelters and a washhouse with two outside toilets. Behind them was the old graveyard wall. At the side of the building on Shettleston Rd. there was another air raid shelter. Across the road was the

Railway Tavern. The two at the graveyard wall had their bricked-up doorways opened partially, and the weans used to use them as dens.

My Da used to work in the shipyards in Clydebank and I'm sure the reason we moved, was that he managed to get a job in the local ropework that was round in Annick St. It ran behind a wall next to our building. If he missed the alarm on the clock that was fast, he could still make his work on time as it was only five minutes' walk.

All the plusses were there, saving on travelling time and bus fares. As he had another mouth to feed. The other thing it was possibly because my Ma was brought up in Annick St., and that most of her family stayed in the east end as well as her best friend. Whereas my Da spent his early life in Bridgeton, and in later years with his Aunty Maggie who also lived in Shettleston.

I'm not quite sure how my parents met but I think my Ma used to go for a walk down

Shettleston Rd. with her pal Lizzie Ferguson, and maybe that's when my Da saw her, while hanging about at street corners further down the road with his pals.

Simulated view from our single end in the early 50's

The old Kirkhouse Inn
2023

The Kirkhouse Building 1930's.
Our house just above the pub.
Picture courtesy of the Kirkhouse Pub

AMONG THE GRAVESTONES

The Kirkhouse 2023

The church at corner of Annick St
and Old Shettleston Rd. to the left

THE OLD BUILDING

One of the first memories that comes to mind is, I was lying in what appeared to be my pram and various people looking in and making all different kinds of baby talk. I don't know why but I seem to think my pram was outside a fruit shop, that was at the corner of Academy St. in Shettleston.

After doing a bit of research, I found it was called Ballantyne fruit and veg. They also had a horse and cart and stayed in a flat above the shop. I must have come to this conclusion because my Ma used this shop quite a lot.

One-time I was playing outside the close that ran through the middle of our building. I was digging in the dirt making roads for my wee cars and I found a box of matches that had been buried. It must have been during the summer because they were dry.

I struck one having seen my Ma and Da using them, and it lit. Getting a fright I dropped it into the box setting fire to the whole box. Between being dirty and smelling of matches, I stayed out my Ma's road. I had learnt my lesson to stay away from them.

I remember my Ma took me through to see one of the neighbours who lived at the back of the building. He asked her to bring me round to see him. His name evades me, but the old man was blind. I imagine that he had not been that way all his life as he had a box with lots of dinky motors in it.

So I guess he must have had sight previously, or maybe there were children at some point. He told my Ma I could have them. I felt all my Christmases had come at once. I ended up back in the dirt again making roads for my trucks and cars, spending numerous hours playing with them.

I spent a lot of my time in what we called the lobby, I used to jump into the coal bunker close the lid and eat the coal. I don't know how I started it, But I couldn't stop. Anytime my Ma was busy I would be right in there. Eventually she caught me, I don't know if the coal wasn't lasting as long, or that It kept disappearing that she realised something was amiss.

She dragged me out of the bunker and took one look at me, and yelled "whit are ye daeing in there, look at the colour of ye". My face was black, so were my teeth. She took me to the doctors the next day, a Dr.Miller if I remember right. She worriedly told him what I had been up to and what did he think. He replied, " It will not do him any harm, but can you afford it?".

I used to go through the close and climb up the middle set of stairs at the back of the building with a small parachute that my Da had made for me. On my way out of the close I passed Mrs. Dempsey who was hanging out the window gabbing to a group of women. I think they were all running down their men and having a laugh.

My parachute consisted of a hanky with four pieces of string at each corner and an old bolt or nut at the end to give it weight. After throwing it over the railings, I would be up and down those stairs repeatedly. At the same time I would be watching the boys that were older than me jumping the gap between the air raid shelter and the toilets, then the smaller gap to the washhouse. It was only the bigger boys that jumped the shelter. I was too wee. From these stairs you could also see beyond the air raid shelters and the gravey wall if anybody was playing football.

Back to the lobby again, our wee porch mirrored another one at the other end of the building, with doors facing each other. Peggy McAloon stayed there. I must have been a bit older now because I bought a sling (catapult) from one of the shops. I thought I would devise my version of chap door run away, only I was doing it through our letterbox with my sling.

I would load up the sling and fire it through the letter box at Peggy's door. I closed it and then opened it a little bit slowly to see if she answered it, she did and looked around to see if she could see anybody and then shut the door. I did it again, shut and slowly opened it a little, she opened her door again to find no one there. Now Peggy was a hardworking wee wummin and fit. I repeated it again, only this time when I eased it open, there she was marching towards our front door.

I scarpered into the living room and hid under the bed. My Ma didne see me I was that fast. When my Ma answered the door Peggy let her have it, "That bloody boy of yours has been belting my door with stones". My Ma didnae (didn't) know what she was on about. The things I put her through.

I remember my Da telling me what happened to him one early morning when he was going to the toilet on the other side of the building. It had no lights and was freezing when you sat down. "It was cold and dark and eerie, and when I put the key into the toilet door, a big black cat jumped on me and scratched me, what a bloody fright I got," he said. Needless to say it didn't take him long in the toilet. Till the day he died he never did like cats.

The old building sat in its own piece of ground, like a big detached with all these different families sharing it with their own wee houses. It was a wee community set back from the main road. Most of the other tenements were just closes and backs where the midgie bins were kept. Speaking of bins, I remember when the midgie men would come to empty them.

Now that was a hard and very dirty job then, they used to wear hats with a neck and shoulder covering to help protect their backs. I'm sure it didn't offer much protection, as those square bins were made of metal and must have been heavy. There was dust everywhere when they emptied them, with the remnants of ashes from the coal fires that were used all throughout the building. They certainly worked for their wages then.

Between the side of building and air raid shelter at Shettleston Rd. was where we had our bonfire on Guy Fawkes night. These fires were sometimes as high as twelve feet. On the lead up to it the weans would all collect wood and various things to throw on it every year. With it being my birthday, I felt really special and would kid myself they had done it all for me.

Some bigger kids used to jump over the fire as it started to die down. I did this when I was older. They used to throw bangers (squibs) at each other. If only the parents knew what their kids got up to when they weren't there. It was not the first time that the fire brigade turned up to put it out. I think my Da used to call them the Burts.

The same place behind air-raid shelter at Shettleston Rd. was where the illegal bookie used to stand and take bets. I'd been told he was the father of a well known Third Lanark football player, that I used to pester for his autograph if I'd see him coming out of the Kirkhouse where he used to drink. He must have thought to himself, oh no, him again. I don't know what happened to the autographs.

When the old building was condemned and vacated, it turned into a free for all with the kids that still lived in the area. They would take pot-shots at the windows that hadn't already been smashed. While running amok through the houses that the doors had been broken into. It portrayed a skeleton of memories. Most of the families had been moved to Easterhouse.

Outside the old building
My Aunty Bridget, Cousin Gerald,
My Ma and Da
Cousin Margaret, myself,
and Cousin Bridie

TOM LAIRD

THE GRAVEY

This is what the kids used to call the old graveyard, that lay over the wall that ran behind the two air raid shelters. On the building side it was about three to four feet high, but on the other side of the wall it was about a six-foot drop onto grass in the graveyard. I can't remember what age I was when I found myself tall enough to get up onto the low side.

But I can recall the ground being higher between the shelter and the wall. Someone had also put a couple of bricks on the ground to assist smaller children to climb over it. Getting down from the wall on the other side was another matter, you could dreep down into the grass or walk along the wall at the ropework side and right along to the end at the red tenement building where it was a lot lower.

The kids spent a lot of time here, between playing games like hide and seek, tig and kick the can. On the centre of the graveyard was a sort of oval/circular area that was gravel. Here we used to play football. We were only kids and there was no disrespect, it was all very innocent.

In the summer the parks department used to send out men, and a beautiful big Clydesdale horse with a red and green cart to cut and collect the grass. They would use scythes to do this. This usually would take two or three days. They couldn't take all the grass at once, so they would pile it into haystacks.

The kids had a field day. We used to jump or somersault off the gravey wall into the haystacks. We did this after they had finished for the day. After they completed, it was back to normal football and games. Sometimes we would have to scatter when the alarm was raised that the Polis (Police) were coming over the wall.

I don't remember anyone getting caught. The gravey had some right old tombstones, so much so that they were worn away. I'm sure they were not all sandstone. A few if I recall were partly marble.

My Ma told me the two rectangular boxes, were sentry boxes at either side of the gates at the main entrance, to deter any grave robbing that must have occurred at that time when the burial ground was opened.

She also told me when she was in her teens, she worked as a housekeeper in a property near Gartocher Rd. near the cemetery. She also said there was a lot of comings and goings especially at night, by horse driven coaches. With carriage lamps swaying from side to side caused by the movement of the coaches it all was very strange and eerie.

She maintained it was something to do with grave robbing, although I think this stopped in mid to late 19th century.

AMONG THE GRAVESTONES

I only found out recently the gravel part of the cemetery was where the Kirk stood. Hence the name of the local inn at that time was the Kirkhouse.

It wasn't always fun and games, sometimes there were fights amongst the kids. I had been involved in some myself. One-time, bigger boys picking fights with me, but because they were older, they would encourage a person halfway between our ages to try to get me to fight.

I didn't like fighting, but if I had to I would. If I was backed into a corner with no way out, I would explode, hence the nickname they gave me was The Atom, something to do with the bomb I expect, or maybe because I was on the small side.

Along at the red building where there were big boulders and concrete rocks, I think that had been dumped from refurbishing the ropework. One day I was off school, and it was a holiday of obligation. Meaning a day celebrating a saint, and catholic schools were given the day off.

It was obligatory to attend. Usually I would go with my Ma, but for some unknown reason she didn't go that day. I dogged it (missed the chapel), I had better things to do, meaning playing among the rocks. If my memory is correct, I was chasing a rabbit which disappeared into a crevice between two rocks which I tried to move, and it rolled back jamming my finger.

I let out an almighty yell, but I managed to lift it again and release it. It had partially crushed it and tore the skin back. I began to feel sick and faint and broke out into a cold sweat. It was at this point that I promised God I would never miss chapel again. I thought he had punished me. Needless to say in later years I never kept my word.

Quite often these rocks served as a battleground where we used to throw stones at each other. We were all pals usually, but we had our fallouts. I can't think of anybody getting seriously hurt at any point, but I do remember a lot of near misses.

It must have been when they were moving the rocks on a tipper lorry, that I was standing on the loose soil embankment which had been built up.

I was watching the lorry tipping his load, and the embankment gave way as he was reversing, and I fell a short distance from his rear wheels, I was on my back and I couldn't get up in time. I don't know who shouted at the driver to stop, but they saved my life, that was another escapade my Ma didn't know about.

I don't know how many times I was nearly knocked down, trying to cross the road to Forbes the Newsagent. There was a time I borrowed a bike from a boy I knew, and while coming down Stepps Rd. the brakes failed, and a lorry had to brake to avoid me. I ran into a fence and crashed his bike. It was damaged so badly that I had to push it backwards to get it home. The boy wasn't very happy, but I told him it wasn't my fault because the brakes were faulty.

Industrial units behind the graveyard where The Ropework stretched all the way back to Annick St.

The old building stood behind the wall at the left-hand side of the graveyard.
It is now the pub car park.

THE MUCK

The place we called the muck was two sort of flattened out hill areas with a broad valley running between them. Both had gravel and grass on top that ran down the sides to the valley. One was 25ft to 30ft high, whereas the other one was lower, probably about 9ft high. Both had football pitches.

The lower one had an old, corrugated arc shaped shed. It resembled an aircraft hangar or air raid shelter. It was pretty big. We sometimes used this as football changing rooms. The pitch on this one was used to play our home games for St. Paul's school.

The other hill not only had gravel on top, but part of one side that ran down sloping to the valley had a big area of gravel. This must have been exposed over the years with the kids sliding down it on cardboard. So I guess these hills must have been spoil heaps from somewhere, possibly from the railway sidings that ran alongside here.

Another possibility might have been from local iron works or mining that occurred in the east end, and that might have been the source. There was also a tile factory at one point I believe. I just don't think they were natural. Most of our days were spent between here and the graveyard. I don't think a summer went by without someone setting fire to the grass.

The Muck ran from Annick St. to Gartocher Road in the east. Sometimes people used it as a shortcut to Shettleston railway station. It was a great place for playing cowboys and Indians, chasing rabbits catching bees and wasps. There is a bee we called a bakey, I don't know why but it had a yellow spot on its head, which we found out through catching them, that it couldn't sting. You could catch them with your hand without any fear.

Sometimes if you thought you had seen a yellow mark you soon found out about it, after catching the bee in your hand you would get stung. Quite often it was down to luck. Another thing we used to chase was butterflies. It was usually the white ones. Once in a while we would see a red one that we were told was a Red Admiral and it was worth a lot of money, £100.00 comes to mind.

When I think back to then kids could unintentionally be cruel, catching bees and imprisoning them in jam jars with airholes in them, thinking you were doing them a favour, by putting some flower cuttings in the in beside them to keep them happy. Not forgetting chasing rabbits and trying to catch them. But again it was all innocently done, and no harm intended.

To think I used take the bees home in a jar, and keep them under the bed. Next day I would go back out to the muck and release them. My poor Ma and Da, what they put up with from me.

The Muck was situated beyond the wall on the right-hand side of the graveyard. It has long gone to the development of Annick Industrial Estate and the private Eastbank Housing Estate at the Gartocher Rd. End.

AMONG THE GRAVESTONES

My Ma's brother Josie
Bottom row 3rd right
I believe this is the higher
part of the Muck

THE CASTLES

The Castles was a name the kids called a big mansion in Sandyhills. It was situated between the prefabs, (post war prefabricated houses) and Sandyhills golf course. We used to have great times here between climbing trees and hiding in the Rhododendron bushes, I can't remember if we had access to the actual house, but I don't think so. It was full of mystique for me. I don't really know if we were supposed to be there, because it was left to grow wild.

The other thing we'd get up to was stealing apples from the houses that were near the adjacent lane. Another adventure was breaking through the fence and following the burn that flowed through the back gardens of Sandyhills and Tollcross all the way to Wellshot Road and Tollcross Park. It gave us more opportunities of finding Apple trees.

It was like an expedition, fighting your way through the vegetation and bushes whilst trying not to fall in the burn. They were happy days, and each day was never the same.

Seemingly the Castles Estate was gifted to Glasgow Corporation, and in the 60's they built four high rise blocks of flats that overlooked the whole of Sandyhills and could be seen from a lot of the Shettleston and Tollcross area.

SANDYHILL FLATS SKETCH

View from Balbeggie St.

Sandyhill Flats view from the golf course at Killin St.

THE SUGAROLLY MOUNTAINS

The Sugarlolly Mountains was a place up in Cranhill. I guess the locals gave the place its title, but that was the name my Ma knew them by, as well as all my pals. They were actually slagheaps that were very high and very steep' These were like Mt Everest compared to our Ben Nevis down at The Muck.

I believed they were from the mining that was previously active but have since found out it was chemical waste. Whether that's the explanation for the gravel at the muck. I think there had been a lot of mining activity round about the east end.

Funny enough with us going into other kids territory, I don't remember any fighting or anything. All you had to do was take a bit of cardboard with you. We were all there just trying to enjoy ourselves.

The other place that was nearby was the Monkland Canal, which was later redeveloped for the M8 motorway, but I can't recall going anywhere near it, except when I was with my cousin Thomas while walking to his house up in Ruchazie.

Tragically he was knocked down by a bus in Gartloch Rd. I think he was about seven or eight. I remember the funeral. There were a lot of people from Ruchazie in attendance.

Cranhill Flats
(Sugarolly Mountains)

THE QUARRIES

Sandyhills golf course was situated between The Castles and Mount Vernon. Sometimes in the summer we'd get a drink from the outside tap that was there for watering the greens. We used it on our way to the quarries that lay either side of Hamilton Road. Both quarries were full of water.

The first one was just behind Kings the motorcycle showroom that is now Arnold Clark. This was all filled in and now used for parking a lot of their stock. The other quarry was on the other side of Hamilton Road. This one was later turned into a dump for the council. In later years more car showrooms were also built here.

Many a day was spent either using large wooden cable drums to use as boats on the first quarry or watching the Sand martins coming and going from their burrows in the sand dunes, as this had been a sand quarry previously. One day the cable drum wouldn't take my weight and started to sink as it drifted from the side.

I panicked and leaped for the edge, trying to grab any vegetation. I didn't quite make it and was fully immersed in the water. After pulling myself out my pal and I lit a fire to dry myself off. That's another episode my Ma didn't know about.

We tried to catch frogs, newts, and lizards in the second one. The water in this one wasn't as deep as the first one. I cut my ankle on broken glass while hunting for newts and lizards. It didn't require stitches, but it ended up septic and I had to have it treated. It left me with a scar. This quarry was more like a wildlife reserve compared to the first one which really just a big hole.

I only found out in later years that there were fish in it, apparently some workmates used to catch trout in it. I went over to it years later to find that the council had started to fill it in and came back with a couple of world war II gasmasks, which my wife threatened to throw me out with them. The M74 now runs at the back of where the second quarry had been.

The first quarry in the golf course was situated behind Arnold Clark's showroom, which was then Kings Motorcycles

The second quarry was later filled in
By the council somewhere behind Motorpoint.

THE STORY

When I eventually was big enough to get over the gravey wall, I would climb over and dreep down (lower myself) if I'd see any other kids playing at football. During school days, it would be as soon as I finished school and got a jeely piece (slice of bread with jam) from my Ma, I'd be right over that wall.

It all depended how many were there that decided the size of the team. You would be playing away and someone else would appear over the wall and they'd have to pick teams all over again. Only this time if they were a better player than you, it meant you would be dropped and put into the other team.

The teams were all shapes and sizes, and a mixed gender. One of the regular players was a girl called Mary. Her brother Alex asked if she could join us. It turned out she was better than some of the boys. She was quite sturdy and would not hesitate to knock you out of the way if needed.

On the opposite end of the spectrum was this wee boy called David. A cracking wee player, he would run rings around most of the team. He was related to my pal Davy and later on in years I believe he signed for Leeds United. An example of raw talent, at the age of five.

Sometimes an argument would start if a decision went the wrong way, as there were no referees, some people were not happy. This would lead to confrontation, sometimes fisticuffs. Needless to say even with referees in a professional capacity nowadays the same thing happens.

The goalposts would be somebody's jacket or jumper each side serving as posts at either end. Many a time on return to their houses and being questioned by their Ma, as to why their clothes were so dirty.

The length of the football games would depend on how many players disappeared for their tea, and if there was enough left to continue. Either that or too much arguing and fighting, as well as if whoever owned the ball went away. The other deciding factor would be the Polis popping their heads over the wall and we would all scarper when the alarm was raised. They never caught us.

The only time I was caught with them, was when we were playing around in my pal Davy's back court, and for some reason the Polis came into the back. Needless to say again we all ran, only this time I climbed over the railings that separated the neighbouring backs and my trousers got tangled up in the top part of them. I was hanging there upside down and I felt a big hand on my collar.

"Well son whit are ye up to" he said at the same time grabbing my leg and unhooking me from the railings. "We were only trying to catch some pigeons mister" looking up at him pleadingly, I knew how to put on a sorry face. "Well son that's not allowed. Don't dae it again, aff ye go and stay oot of trouble". I walked away at first slowly and then instinctively ran.

I think it was Davy's neighbour across the close on the ground floor who reported us. She must have seen us from her back window, loosen a bobbin of thread amongst the grass and throwing bread down in between the sparse tangle. It certainly worked because we caught a few pigeons. She used to spy on us a lot, I think she thought we couldn't see her.

Davy stayed in a corporation house up the road from us between Bell the newsagent and further up was Mary Macks the sweetie shop. The back of his building was separated by a wall that faced on to the Muck. On his side of the wall there was also an air-raid shelter. Only this one was a different shape to ours. It had a concrete roof that comprised of three or four arches. An Anderson type shelter, I believe.

I remember being on it once and losing my balance and sliding off it on my back upside-down landing on the ground with an almighty thud. I tried to yell but I couldn't. My voice was stuttering coming out in dribs and drabs.

I think the shock to my spine was the problem. It was about two or three minutes before I was talking properly, although it felt a lot longer. I thought I wouldn't be able talk again, although it might have made a few people happy.

The concrete air-raid shelter,
Davy's back yard

THE SKI JUMP

Speaking of Bell's the newsagent I used to go in there from time to time to buy a packet of crisps. It wasn't the first time that the contents were like rubber. I think it was due to dampness in the shop or being old stock. It was so bad once when I opened the wee blue salt packet, it was a single lump all stuck together, you needed a hammer to break it.

This brings me to the time I was looking in their shop window, and they had started selling a few toys, there was a skier at the top of a supposedly ski jump. It was made of tinplate with a key that, when wound up started the mechanism and made him jump and ski down a chute. I had never seen anything like this before.

I ran round to the ropework in Annick St. to wait for my Da coming out at five o clock, I used to meet him a lot when he finished. All the way round to our house I kept going on about this ski jump. He then asked me how much it was, "Its only 3/9p" I replied with a wee sob threw in here and there. "Oh no that's too dear" he said in a loud voice.

That equated to about just over a fifth of a pound. Now at that time I believe my Da only earned about £9.00 a week without overtime. That night I gret and I gret (cried and cried) nonstop. "The shop shuts at hauf past eight ," (half past eight) I would cry. It was relentless.

I don't know how my Da never gave me a good skelp (slap) for all that persistent crying. Finally he gave in, he got up and went to the kitchen cabinet where he kept his money. "Here go and get it, the shop is still open" he growled. Needless to say, with my heavy handedness it didn't last more than several months.

Another time I was walking along the Gravey wall at the ropework side, and I fell off it and split my head open. I don't know how I did it, but I must have stood on something and managed to get myself up onto the wall again. It was bleeding badly. I could hardly see where I was going through the blood, but I made it back to our house.

It was a Sunday which was my Da's day off. Reluctantly I went through the door where my Da was sitting reading the Sunday paper. "Good god, no that wall again" he shouted. He knew I was never off it, because if his workmates were working down at the graveyard end of the rope work, they would see me and they would tell him.

"Whit are we gonnae dae, that'll need stitches, right I'll take you up to Doctor Sadler's house in Killin Street, to see if he can help us". The doctor wasn't even our doctor, but my Da grabbed my hand and said, "Let's go". On arriving at the house and ringing the front doorbell which was duly answered by the doctor himself.

"Oh dear, what's happened here", without any hesitation. "Bring him in, I'll have to stitch that" he said. He probably used some sort of local anaesthetic, but it didn't feel like it at the time, I'll never forget it. My Da offered the doctor money, which he refused to take. My Da, thanked him again and encouraged me to do so as well.

One of the other times that I fell off the wall was when Tommy my pal and I were walking along it and we lost our balance. I don't know which one of us grabbed on to the other, but we both fell at the same time. I think Tommy escaped a bad injury because I was the reason that the ambulance was called.

By the time it arrived, it looked as if I was concussed, because I was lying with my eyes closed. It turned out I had chipped my elbow bone. My Ma was so relieved, she would tell anybody that would listen about my concussion. It was only later, much later (In my early forties) that I chose to tell her I was pretending I was sleeping. I was too feart to open them. In case I got a belt from my Ma or Da.

She couldn't believe it, all those years she used to tell the story how I was taken away in the ambulance suffering from concussion. It's amazing how brave forty odd years further on can make you.

Ambulance outside the Gravey

COWBOYS AND INDIANS

We used to play at cowboys and Indians quite often. When you were a cowboy, you would have a Lone Star gun that fired repeating ceps, (little paper rolls with individual spots of powder, that banged when the hammer of the pistol struck them) with a holster to match, and of course a western waistcoat and cowboy hat with a chinstrap. This meant it didn't blow off when you were running and kidding on you were riding your horse.

On the other hand if you were a red Indian, you would stick a feather in your hair and some dirt rubbed into the face or add some sort of colour. If you were lucky you'd maybe get a hold of it from your sisters, that is if they didn't see their lipstick getting smaller. As far as weapons went, we would make our own bows and arrows from bamboo canes and the green sticks that were used for supporting plants.

We used to get these from Knox's the hardware shop just past Academy St. on Shettleston Rd. I think it was his brother that owned the newsagents/confectioner that used to be at the corner of Gartocher Rd. The canes were picked for their length, not too long or too short. It cost only pennies to make up your bow including 4 or 5 arrows.

You would cut a slot at each end. This would accommodate the string that slotted into it and then you would wrap around it several times, bending the cane, and slotting it into the other end when the right tension was achieved, wrapping it again several times around it and tying it off. Finishing off both ends covering the string with a coating of varnish or similar to seal and protect them.

The green sticks that would be the arrows were sharpened at one end and the thick rubber bands that you got from the screw top in the stoppers in Irn Bru bottles, (**Although I seem to remember seeing labels spelt Brew, I think that this spelling was intended not to be used after 1946, old labels maybe!)** and twisted it three times about an inch from the point. Doing this balanced the arrow making them very effective. You could fire them quite a distance, but these arrows were actually very dangerous.

On one occasion when we were playing, I was a cowboy hiding from the Indians, all of a sudden there was an almighty thud to the side of my face. I had been spotted by one of the Indians. What I didn't realise that there was an arrow sticking out of my cheek, which was when the pain kicked in. The wee red Indian that fired it came running towards me screaming repeatedly "I'm sorry". When he reached me he had a look at it and tried to remove it, but the rubber stopper prevented him from pulling it out.

It had to be removed in the opposite direction exiting through my mouth. Unbelievably there wasn't much blood. I had to go back and face my Ma who was at the end of her tether with me. If only she had seen it when the arrow was sticking out of my cheek, that's another scar I had acquired.

One summer a bigger boy who was playing at being an Indian over in the muck at the top of the highest hill tried sending smoke signals and accidently set the grass on fire. Most of the side the of hill ended up burning before it was put out by all of us who were playing there that day.

It must have been a Saturday because my Ma told to come back to the house before 4.00pm. She had to get me cleaned and dressed as we were going to a wedding reception for 6.00pm in the Cooperative Halls in Pettigrew St. Shettleston.

When she saw me she tried not to blow a fuse. I was reeking of smoke and my eyes and face were black. My eyes were all red with rubbing them. You could say I was a sight for sore eyes.

My sister Ellen's boyfriend George, who was a carpenter made me a wooden sword and shield, the sword was almost as tall as me. The first time I went over the muck with it, all my pals ran away, I must have terrorised them.

Another time he made me a flying model of a Spitfire or a Hurricane with an elastic band propeller to power it. Unfortunately it lasted 2 or 3 attempts before crashing to the ground and destroying it. It must have taken him a long time to make it, being built from balsa wood and the fuselage covered in some sort of cloth and painted. I can't imagine what he must have thought when he saw it was ruined.

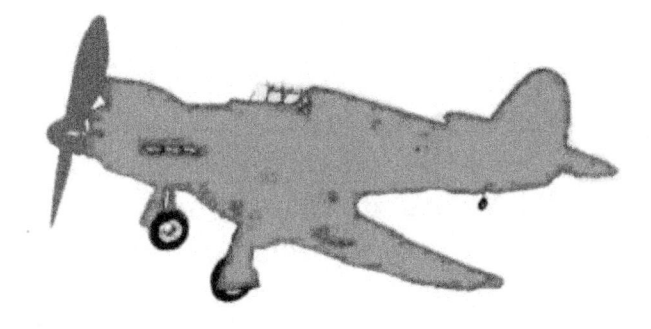

The plane George built for me.

THE BLUEBELL WOODS

Sometimes we would decide to visit the Bluebell Woods at the other side of Mount Vernon. On our way there we used to pass what we called the army dump that was situated in a field between Barlanark and Baillieston Rd. Although I would have liked to see inside it I never got the chance to do it.

We would cross the road to Sandyhills Road and pass the prefabs on the right-hand side. Mount Vernon was a lot smaller then. It didn't take us too long before we reached open countryside. There was one particular field that was our favourite. One, which the farmer grew potatoes in..

We would sneak into the field and dig up two or three and disappear into the woods and light a fire to cook them. Whenever we thought they had plenty of time over the flames or they were charred enough, we'd pierce them with a twig and remove them.

Trying not to burn our fingers or mouth, the anticipation overcame the fear of taking a bite. Sinking our teeth through the burnt skin it did not disappoint. They might have been hard, but they were free. Finishing off with blackened teeth we would head back home.

On returning home I would try to get to the sink to wash my mouth and teeth before my Ma saw me, but that's hard in a single end. She'd ask was I thirsty and where I had been, with me spluttering out "Aye Ma jist oot wi my pals." Quite often she would take me up to visit her sister Sissie who lived in Barlanark.

On the way there we would walk up towards Barrachnie where we'd pass the field where my pals and me would get the potatoes. "Lovely up here, I should bring you up here more often" she said. "Aye Ma" I replied.

I remember my auntie Sissie had a big piano in her living room, I don't know who played it, but I was thinking I'd like to try it. At one time there was a big rocking horse in one of bedrooms it was as tall as me, and I was allowed, to sit on it once. They didn't have it for long, It might have been sold as they did not have any children and her man was a rag and bone man.

He'd a horse and cart, which quite often he would come into our building looking for rags and clothes. He would hand out balloons in exchange for these. We always knew when he was there. There was one helluva racket that came out his brass trumpet.

My aunt had an au pair, It must have been because her health wasn't too good. Her name was Gertrude, and she was German. Considering it must have been only about eight years after the end of the war in 1945, I think she might have a had tough time of it.

When my aunt Sissie died, we attended a service in the house, and her husband lifted me up to see her in her coffin after me telling him I didn't want to. It was the first dead person I had ever seen. Ending on that, who would have thought a rag and bone man would have had an au-pair.

In later years, it must have been after I started secondary school, sometimes my Ma used to give me any old clothes she was throwing out, and I would take them down Old Shettleston Rd. to a rag merchant that had an old ramshackle hut on some spare ground where they paid me cash.

It must have been near Darlieth St. because I remember after getting the money, I went to a shop that was around the corner on Shettleston Rd. that sold shirts and ties, and treated myself to a Slimjim tie that cost 4/6d (four shillings and sixpence) for those of you who haven't a clue what I am talking about.

It was a blue and black tie that was only about an inch wide with diagonal stripes. I got it to to go with one of my air force blue shirts which was my facourite colour of shirt. So you could say I was in the rag trade myself.

Ragman's horse and cart

MARBLES & CONKERS

Playing marbles was a bit of a skill, you needed a pretty good aim to play. The idea behind the game was to knock your opponent's bool or Jorrie (marble) out of the area of a ring that was marked in the soil. You had to knock his out and at the same time keep yours in. At the end of the game, any you knocked out you kept, same went for your opponent.

Each person usually had one particular bool that they considered it as their lucky one. If you lost that one or if it was damaged it was a big loss and was felt it could affect your play. When I say damaged I mean chips out of the bool made by either bigger ones or ball bearings that were unfair but allowed. My Da's cousin's husband used to work in the steel works in Cambuslang.

Anytime we went up to visit them, he would have a load of ball bearings that he had saved for me. My pals used to dread it if they heard I had been to see my mystery benefactor, who I kept secret. Sometimes we would use to play with them on stanks (square drain cover full of holes) but what the rules were evades me.

One other thing we used to play at if you can call it that was knifey, standing with your feet apart and someone with a penknife would throw it as close to your feet as possible, without touching your shoes. Once in a while it would strike a shoe, but I don't recall anyone getting hurt, once again it was all innocent and naïve.

Back then knives were readily available, all kinds from penknives to sheathed hunting knives. The difference then as far as I can remember there was very little knife crime when I was a child. In later years there was a teenager who had gone to the same primary school as me who was a stabbed fatally by twin brothers, in Shettleston. It reportedly happened in Gartocher Rd.

Conkers was another pastime, which was seasonal, only when you could get them. A chestnut with a length string threaded through it. That and a good set of knuckles. My hand was forever getting walloped by enthusiastic opponents.

A game of marbles

THE PRIEST

I must have been in a fight, or I got a doing from somebody because, I remember going back round to the house and not going in because the priest (Father Glynn) must have been visiting my Ma. His motorbike was parked outside our door, he was the only one I knew who had a motorbike.

Not wanting to disturb her I climbed up onto the window ledge and slowly peeked over the net curtains to see my Ma sitting there facing me talking to the priest who had his back to me. I don't know if she had seen me, but the tears were streaming down my face, I just wanted my Ma.

I don't recall if I went in or I stayed out, but I did see the priest's motorbike a lot. It turns out he asked my Ma if he could park it there so he could go round to the Kirkhouse for a pint, and nobody would be any the wiser. One year he gave me a penlight torch for my Christmas. I played with that torch until the batteries went flat.

I couldn't afford to buy batteries for it so the next time I visited my Da's Auntie Maggie in Pettigrew St., she would let me put the batteries in her oven that was part of the cast iron range cooker which was on most of the time because it backed onto a coal fire. This would work quite a few times before the batteries died. In later years I would be delivering butcher meat to St. Paul's chapel house every Saturday. By that time Father Glynn had been moved on and I know it wasn't The Kirkhouse.

The chapel owned ground behind the chapel house, where they would hold a garden fete every year. They would have things like Tombola and trying to kick a ball through a hole in a wooden cutout to win a prize. Willie Toner the footballer, who stayed in Shettleston, was sometimes in charge of this.

I remember one year I was asked to help out on one of the stalls that was selling various items of bric-a-brac and some toys. I noticed there was a small selection of Triang minic railway train engines, carriages, and some rails. I asked the woman in charge of the stall how much it was and told it would be a shilling. This was before the fete opened, so she kept it for me until I ran down to the house to get the money. I had them for years.

Priest's Motorbike

ST. PAUL'S PRIMARY

I can't recall my first day at school. But I do remember who my first primary teacher was. Mrs. Burns was her name, who was a lovely woman. One day I took a wee toy bird in a cage into class. When you gave it a wee shake it would spring up and down on its perch, making a chirping noise at the same time.

Mrs. Burns asked where I got it from, and I told her my sisters got it for me in the Barras. She then asked if I would ask them if they could get her one if she gave me the money. Well my sisters managed to get one the same as mine, and she was over the moon with it.

I remember one summer my Ma and Da went away for the day to Girvan, and they brought me back a tin banjo because I had Chickenpox and couldn't go with them. They knew I liked music and singing so much but they soon regretted it.. I would strum it and strum it thinking I was playing some kind of tune. One of my favourites was Bernadine a song by Pat Boone at the time. I would knock hell out of that banjo and belt it out at my loudest, to my parents dismay.

It must have been a couple of years later when my sister Ellen's boyfriend at the time, (Future brother-in-law), gave me a proper Spanish acoustic guitar. After a bit of practice, I mentioned to my teacher in St. Pauls that I had this guitar that I was given and could play it. She invited me to bring it into the class and play it for them.

Well the day arrived, and I proudly carried my guitar in its lovely vinyl case all the way up to school, which was about a 10-to-15-minute walk, depending on the speed of your walk, (dilly dally or normal). Well after waiting for the school bell to ring and go into the classroom, after roll call the teacher invited me up to play.

Well class Thomas is going to give us a song. There was no holding me back, I got up there and got stuck right into Bernadine, which sounded just like it did when I played the banjo. She let me continue for what must have been a couple of minutes or so, I don't know because I was lost in my music. Right Thomas that was lovely, okay class show your appreciation, I remember hearing a few stuttered claps. That was my first and last public performance with the guitar.

Sometimes during music lesson and singing songs in the class, the teacher used to tell me to take a wee rest so I would not damage my vocal chords. I think I was too enthusiastic, as I really liked singing, either that or she thought I was rotten.

When I used to go to the Saturday morning matinee at the Odeon Shettleston I entered the singing competition, twice singing Fats Domino's Blueberry Hill. I won it the first time and came second the next. Whether it was won on merit or because seemingly there were some children in the audience that knew me who made the loudest noise when asked to vote. Those were the days.

I used to love playing football as I said earlier in the book. As I progressed through the classes, as I got to the two higher classes age wise, we had a new teacher, Mr. Keegan was his name, and he used to run the school team. So part of the curriculum was playing football. The pitch was round the back of the school with an adjacent high wall, where there was an egg factory I believe, on the other side. I just thought I would mention that.

Even with my small stature I was given the position of left back, I think it was because if anybody came running at me I wouldn't flinch and just blocked them and ran away with the ball. He did try me in another position at outside left with me being left footed it was ideal.

I managed to score a few goals, being a bit of a poacher not understanding the offside rule but that was my favourite position. Anyway my first school team outing I was given left back position. I do remember my Da taking me into the Barras for football boots. Unfortunately they were second hand and didn't fit right and were uncomfortable. They wouldn't stop me from playing.

We played our home games over in the muck, and I used to love it when my Da would come over from the house and watch me play. My last game for the school should have been an away game to St. Roch's school in Royston. It was a Saturday morning, and I was supposed to meet the team at a bus stop in High St. at about 8.45 am.

That morning when I woke up and realised it was raining, I decided not to go, my Da lectured me about being a fair-weather player and told me I was letting the team down. I still don't know why I didn't go as I would play in all kinds of weather. Needless to say when I went to school on Monday morning, Mr Keegan pulled me in right away and told me not only was I dropped, but I would never play again for the school.

The games we used to play in the playground include Tig and Dodgy. On one occasion while playing dodgy with a tennis ball, I threw it at someone and missed. It went straight through a small pane of glass in one of the classrooms. When the playtime break was over I was going to report it to our teacher, but one of the girls in our class beat me to it.

I was sent to the headmaster and received a telling off. At the time it was a huge thing to happen to me, but looking back it put it into perspective it was just a wee accident. My best pals in the primary were Jim, Wullie, and Philip.

TOM LAIRD

St. Pauls 1956 APPROX.
Myself, 1 in from left, 2nd row.
Top to bottom.

THE SEASIDE

My Ma and Da liked going away for the day down the coast to one of the many resorts on the Clyde coast. Usually it was a caur (Tramcar) into the town to one of the three stations where my Da would buy a cheap day return for us. A favourite was Ayr.

I think the reason for this was because My Da was stationed at Ayr racecourse that used to be barracks for the army during the war, My Ma used to always say he wisny in the war, It was a holiday he was on. It usually was a tossup whether it was Ayr or Saltcoats.

One year they went to Girvan and brought me back a banjo which I already mentioned, and It didn't take long for them to realise, how big a mistake it was. I used to play that wee banjo any chance I got. It was the same racket for every song, they all sounded the same. As I said My Da loved the coastal resorts, and when I got older they started going bus trips, that the local bus operator ran 2 or 3 times a week.

On one such trip, it was a bus run to Callander in the Trossachs, a lovely town, but it was not his cup of tea. Every now and then they would run a mystery tour. Great, my Da thought, this is something different, Something new. They would put an advertising board out each week, listing the tours. My Da spotted that this was one of these new mystery tours listed on the board.

Straight in he went and booked it. Two days later they were on the bus. This is great Annie, we don't know where we're going, I like a surprise. The bus made its way out into the country, up and down hills past lochs and lovely scenery. "I wonder when we'll get to the coast Annie". "Don't know" my Ma replied. About 15 minutes later made its way into a town.

"Where do you think we are Annie?", "Don't know" she replied. He didn't twig (realise) because the bus came into the town from a different direction. "BLOODY CALLANDER" He blurted out. That was the last mystery tour they ever went. I don't know when, the bus operator, Eastern Scottish, eventually stopped doing them.

My two sisters Sadie and Ellen must have gone down the coast now and then. I think this photo, was taken in Saltcoats or Helensburgh.

Sadie and Ellen

FIRST COMMUNION

The day of my first communion was on a Saturday, and my Ma and Da had bought me a burgundy blazer to wear as well as new shorts and a pair of shoes. My Ma was so proud of me she said I should go round and see some of the neighbours and let them see me. Now I don't know if it was tradition or the neighbours being nice, but I accumulated quite a bit of money. I was rich.

After the communion service we jumped on a caur (Tramcar) down to Bridgeton to get my photo taken before I ruined the look. The photographers I believe was called the State Studios Bridgeton Cross where a nice photo was taken. We then went along to the barras where I was given the chance to pick a new Jerkin. I wanted one of the new ones that were out at the time.

I think it was made of imitation leather (rexine). It was the same as the one the cops wore in the TV series Highway Patrol featuring Broderick Crawford. As soon as I got it I put it straight on. My blazer was put into a bag that my Ma had brought with her. They must have had this surprise all planned.

From there it was on to the sweetie shop and the Olympia Picture House back along at Bridgeton Cross. I couldn't tell you what picture was showing because I was too busy admiring my jerkin. Despite all the attempts by my Ma, I wouldn't take it off, even though the sweat was running off me. So I suffered with a wee smile on my face. I don't remember much else that day, but I do know I felt like Broderick Crawford.

CINNAMON STICK

A few of my pals and I were in one of the air-raid shelters to talk about making a Guy (Stuffed Dummy) to put in a pram and try to raise some money (Penny for the guy) to buy fireworks. The other thing we were discussing was where to get wood and things for the bonfire. At the same time the older ones were passing around a lit cinnamon stick pretending it was a cigarette. The smaller weans didn't get a puff at it.

It was the next couple of weeks that we collected money outside the Kirkhouse and the Sheiling further up Shettleston Rd. We tried to avoid running into the weans that stayed at that end because we strayed onto their territory. After all, we were stealing all their potential drunks. Anyway we managed to escape any confrontation. Eventually came the big day my birthday, Guy Fawkes day.

Nobody told us the real reason why this day was special until we went to school. I just know we enjoyed seeing the bonfire getting lit, and seeing the fireworks being set off, Rockets, Catherine Wheels, and Bangers (Squibs). As I had some money of my own because it was my birthday when the supply was getting low, I would run down to the bike shop in Old Shettleston Rd where they always had a supply of penny bangers.

As the fire began to dwindle, sometimes the Burts (Fire Brigade) would turn up to check on the fire. If they were satisfied, off they'd go, and that's when the older kids would start jumping over the fire. I did it once when it got lower. This was all happening out of our parents sight, who had went back to their houses when the fire looked safe. If only they knew.

There was an occasion when the Fire Brigade had to douse it, as it looked as if it would get out of hand, leaving a mess which the corporation removed a couple of days later.

One of my other memories was the man who came round on a three-wheeler bike selling ice cream from what was some kind of fridge. The other one that comes to mind was the onion sellers, complete with French beret, whether they came from France is another question.

Fireman dousing the bonfire.

TOAD IN THE HOLE

By this time we had moved into the building above the Kirkhouse pub. Mr. Forbes who owned the paper shop across the road from the Kirkhouse Pub told my sister Ellen that he wanted to speak to my Da. He told my Da there was a house going to be available upstairs above the pub. My Da quickly followed up the tip and contacted the factor and secured the house for when it would be empty.

The old building that we were moving from had been condemned and had been put under a demolition order and all the occupants were to be moved to the new scheme that was named Easterhouse. My Da was adamant he wasn't going there, and the timing of this could not have been better. After all it was a two room and kitchen with an inside toilet a big improvement to what we had been used to.

It was summer when I was playing over in the muck on the side of hill near where the slag slide was. I noticed this hole that I hadn't noticed before. It was about 3 inches in diameter. I was playing with this other boy. Christopher was his name and he dared me to put my hand in it. Reluctantly I did, my arm went in about up to my elbow when I thought I felt something cold. I immediately pulled it out not knowing what I could have touched.

"What's wrong?" Christopher said. "There's something cold in there." I said in a shocked manner. "Put it back in, you'll be all right" he said in what sounded like an order. He was a good bit older and bigger than me, so I hesitantly obeyed. As I reached into the back of the hole I felt it again and I tried not to withdraw my hand and try to feel what it was. Slowly I closed my grip without squeezing.

I decided to get a hold of it and pull it out. It was only then that I felt it moving, trying to escape my grasp. I softly tightened my grip and withdrew my hand to find a big toad in it. "Wow, that's a beauty, can I hold it?" he eagerly asked. "In a wee while, I want to look at it first" I replied. "Okay if you promise to let me, let's walk along to the station" said Christopher.

The station was only about five minutes away, and I just loved watching the steam trains stopping here. A good vantage point was from the passenger railway bridge crossing, that was a crisscrossed iron design is the best way I can describe it. It was great because you could see through it.

There was a train in at the time and I was totally engrossed with it. "Can I see your toad now, you promised" he said. "okay" was my reply. I was too busy watching the train pull away and he said "Look" as he dropped my toad into the funnel of the train passing underneath.

It must have been that this was the time that he grabbed my throat in our close on the stairs because I wouldn't stop crying at what he had done. He tightened his grip and I struggled, and at the same time was making such a commotion that my Ma must have heard us and opened the door. She shouted at him, and he loosened his hold on me and fled.

It must have been before this happened, that he tried to sell me his electric train set for a pound. He said I could pay it up at sixpence a week over twenty weeks and he would give it to me then, but I never saw him again after the toad episode. I dare say I would never have seen the train set if I had given him my pocket money.

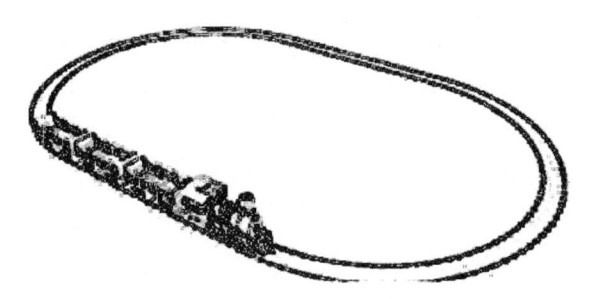

The train that never arrived.

THE WINTER

We kids loved the winter, there were all sorts of things we could do. In the school at playtime, the fog was that thick, that my pals and I were all pretending we were pilots flying our planes through the clouds, it was great fun.

I'm not sure if that was one of the occasions we were sent home because the toilets were frozen, it used to happen on a regular basis. Great!, that gave us more time to pursue our winter pastimes. I had an old sledge that someone gave me. It wasn't one these fancy ones that could sit on and guide it from that position.

No, this one was low to the ground, it was only about 5"-6" high and it had a couple of copper pipes fixed to the bottom for runners. You had to lie-down all the time on your stomach and guide it with your feet. I must have gone through a couple of pairs of shoes doing that, your feet were also used as brakes.

A favourite place was at the burn in Hermiston Rd. Greenfield, it had a wee hill running down from the road to the burn. It didn't take much of a fall of snow to make it a popular venue with the kids. Funny enough, I don't recall The Muck being used for sledging, I think the high hill was too steep.

One late winter's afternoon when it was just about to get dark, my pals turned up at my door saying they had a great place to go sledging. Turned out it was Sandyhills golf course. You went up the lane at the side of Castles estate which brought you out at the gate of the course.

There was a right of way public footpath that we used to go to the quarries in the summer, so the gate to the golf course was always open. There had been a good fall of snow and there was not even a footprint on the course .

It was eerie even with the brightness of the snow in the dark, but we had come a long way with our sledges, so nothing was going to deter us. From the public footpath you could see all the way down the hill to Killin St, and that is where we ended up once we launched ourselves off the hill. It was quite a distance, so we only did it once, it was too far to trudge back up the hill through the deep snow, but it was worth it, even though we had a long trek back home.

Sledging at the golf course

RADIO and TELEVISION

We didn't have a TV until I was about 11, but before that my sister Ellen's boyfriend's mother gave us a radio which I remember listening to, shows like workers playtime and various other things. I was always inquisitive and wanted to know how things worked.

Quite often I would open up the back and look inside at all the various valves that were all lit up, it reminded me of a wee hoose with all the lights switched on. I used to have a wee look to see if everything was as it should be.

As I said I was about 11 or 12 years old when my Da bought a second-hand telly. I can't recall if he got in the barras, or a used furniture shop in Maryhill that he visited quite a lot when he was needing something for the house.

We would all be glued to it especially at the weekends when The Kathy Kirby show or Sunday night at The London Palladium would be on. All was well until the telly stopped working, there was no sound coming from it. Kathy Kirby just wasn't the same with no voice.

It lay that way for what seemed like ages. My Ma and Da didn't know anybody that could fix it, anyway they couldn't afford it. I asked my Ma if I could open up the back of the telly to have wee look. Now nobody was allowed touch that telly apart from my Da. She hesitantly said yes. As long as it was before my Da came in.

I proceeded to remove the back cover and switched the telly on. It lit up like Blackpool Illuminations. I could see that this new-fangled thing had valves as well. I surveyed all of the inside and I noticed one of the valves was not lit. I switched of the telly and removed what I thought was the offending valve.

I was now able to get a good look at it and read the number on it, which seemed familiar. I told my Ma I was going to open up the wireless, she looked at me with that oh god look. Looking into the back I spotted what I was looking for. I was right, it had a valve with the same number.

I removed it and inserted it into the back of the telly. After switching it on all the valves lit up and the sound was back. When my Da came in and found out it was working again I was the hero of the day, I could do no wrong.

So when anything electrical wasn't working, I was the go-to man. It wasn't long after that our electric doorbell stopped working. I asked my Ma if she wanted me to look at it, she said ok. I got the wooden stepladders out, as the box was above the door. I removed the cover and had a good look.

The wires were all connected. I loosened them thinking there was no power going to them, I touched them together to check, BOOM! I was thrown off the ladders against the wall. Fortunately, I was ok and lived to tell the tale. Needless to say I never offered, or was asked again, to fix anything.

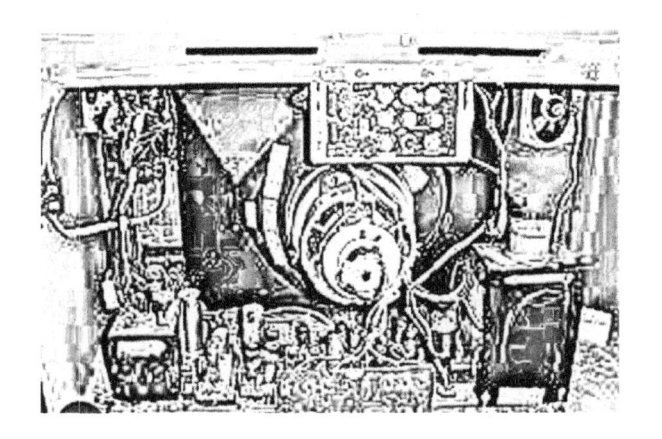

TV with back removed.

Donor Radio

NEW HEIGHTS

At St. Pauls primary when I was about seven or eight, I used to go to a gymnastic class twice a week, I think it was held on Tues. and Thurs. nights. Mr. McGoldrick was the gymnastic teacher, and his two sons attended these classes, as well as about another 20 to 25 boys.

I had never done gymnastics before and was totally immersed in what he was teaching us. We were getting taught various exercises as well as horse box vaulting, head stands, headsprings, handsprings, hand walking which I was hopeless at. His two sons were really good at doing this.

After every class night I would be back down the road by about 9.00 p.m. and my Ma had a plate of Tripe ready for me, it was cooked like a thick soup. I never had it since those days, but I am sure can remember the taste, I loved it. It's funny how things like that never fade.

I remember Mr. McGoldrick asked me if I wanted to take part in a gymnastic display alongside his two sons in the deaf and dumb school in Tollcross, St. Vincent's it was called. This was the first of two occasions that I was in a display, and it went very well.

After several months we were getting more competent and confident. He started training us for a gymnastic display which would be held in the Wellshot Halls (Shettleston Halls) in Wellshot Rd. This would involve disciplined exercises and a Pyramid Display.

Fortunately our pyramid would not involve, standing on shoulders but kneeling on each other's backs. I'm not sure how many tiers there was, but I think it was 5 rows kneeling and the top person, standing.

This may not seem too high, but when you're the one on top, I can assure you it was, especially as the stage was about 6 or 7 feet high, and I know because I was the one selected to be on the top. With me being the smallest and lightest, I assume that was the reasoning. Anyway the finale to the show was the curtains were to open with the pyramid fully assembled with me at the top.

And guess who was sitting in the middle of the front row looking up proudly, was my wee Ma. I used to always kid her on that it was a good job I never fell, as I would have ended up on her lap.

The Pyramid

SHETTLESTON BATHS

A trip to Shettleston baths was always on the agenda. Usually I would go myself or with one of my pals. I remember the first time I visited there, I think it was with one of my pals and his dad, I know it definitely was an adult, and he threw me in knowing I couldn't swim, it was the shallow end, but I panicked, spluttering after swallowing some water. It nearly put me off going back again.

I decided to give it a go again, and someone had given me a pair of flippers to try. After putting them on, I tried to keep my head above the water and move forward. Slowly I began to gain confidence with these on and kept on going. Before long I was actually swimming,

I found I was swimming faster than some of my pals. It was only when I stopped wearing them I realised that they were the reason I was doing so well, and they were keeping me up. I started to sink without them, what they did do was gave me confidence to not be afraid of drowning and learn to swim properly. Eventually I got the hang of it.

There was a Brylcreem machine at the pool, when if you put in a penny, it would ooze a dollop of the cream into your hand. I used to make sure I kept a penny for it, especially in the winter months, it would stop your hair freezing. On the way home, I would maybe scoff down a hot mince pie.

In the summer months it was a different story. On my way back to the house along Shettleston Rd, I would either buy a frozen jubilee or a pear/cider ice lolly. I wasn't keen on the triangular shaped jubilee ones; they were hard to sook. But the ones that were in the box type carton, were better.

When there was no juice left at the top, you could turn it upside down to find it had turned sort of slushy and were great to sook. A favourite choice of ginger (soft drink)) was between Irn Bru, (having previously been spelt as Iron Brew). American Cream Soda, Limeade, and Cider or Pineappleade were options as well.

On the odd occasion I would opt for the healthier choice of pea pods. My Ma always asked why it took me so long to come back from the swimming, not knowing I stopped at nearly every toy shop peering into their windows. In later years when I went to secondary school, swimming was part of the curriculum. The best thing was you didn't have to pay to get in.

As I got older I used the bath facility there. Long gone were the days when my Ma used to give me a right good scrub in the sink of the single end on a Sunday morning. Sometimes with an audience of my female cousins who just happen to coincidently visit around about my bath time.

AMONG THE GRAVESTONES

A SERVICE FOR EVERY MAN

Just what he wants . . **BRYLCREEM**
At the right moment
Just the right amount . .

A SERVICE FOR EVERY BATH

Bringing in revenue – Costing nothing to instal and maintain
Providing a much appreciated service for bathers

Backed By . . . .
A Really Efficient Service System

AUTOMATIC HAIR-CREAM VENDING MACHINES LTD.
HONEYPOT LANE, STANMORE, MIDDLESEX. Tel. WORdsworth 4321

At a penny a pat, pilfering was a perennial problem!

My Da and his Aunt Maggie

THE BOWERY

The Bowery was the far end of Pettigrew St., where the Cooperative creamery was situated as well as the Cooperative Halls across the road. I didn't really venture down that end of the street much.

I tended to stay up at the part where my Da's aunty Maggie lived in Pettigrew St. I sometimes stayed a Saturday through to a Sunday with her. This was where I got to meet my cousins, well that's what I thought, turns out they were my 2nd cousins. You don't really understand that when you are young.

We used to play games Ludo (which was Maggie's favourite) and Snakes and

Ladders, That was about the scope of the selection of the board games. Another popular pastime was playing Snap with the cards or Pontoons. When we ran out of games then we would hold a concert if I remember right.

We sometimes met up at Maggie's hut, that she owned through at Port Seton. After the journey on the bus to Edinburgh, one of my early memories was waiting for the bus in Princes St. at the gardens for the connection to Port Seton. On one occasion there was a lot of people through for the weekend, and all the cousins had to share the same bed. There must have been about five or six of us head to toe to maximise the space in the bed. One in particular used get mischievous with her feet.

One of my Da's cousins Tom, owned a caravan there as well, although I don't remember being in it. A visit to the pig farm that was adjacent to the caravan site was always a must. One of the things Maggie liked to do a lot, was to take a trip to Rhu, just past Helensburgh to collect mussels, and whelks, they would bring them back by the barrowload. Clootie dumplings was another of her favourites and hiding the silver threepenny pieces inside. She always warned us to be careful when eating a piece just in case.

A Sunday seemed to be when a lot of my Da's side of the family met up at Maggie's house usually, and there was a lot of them. The living room always felt overcrowded as there wasn't enough seats, and it was standing room only.

One of his cousins had a big, crooked scar, running down the middle of his head, and I always wondered how he got it, I was too afraid to ask. Maggie's friend/boyfriend reminded me of one of the old silent movie actors, Harold Lloyd, I think it was because he wore same kind of glasses.

.At this end of Pettigrew St. was the Cooperative Milk float depot, and opposite stood the Odeon Picture house. I used to attend the Saturday matinees here, I liked the films, but you could hardly hear them, and every now and then you had to duck to avoid getting hit on the back of the head with all the missiles that were being chucked about. When it got really bad the film would be stopped and the cinema manager would walk onto to the stage and threaten to throw us all out. This usually happened at least twice each visit. He never did throw us out, it was just a threat.

My favourite part of the morning was at half time they would have a singing competition, which I entered twice, I won it the first time, singing Blueberry Hill the Fats Domino song, and the next time I came in second beaten by a girl singing Gypsy Rover. I think she was second to me when I won it. I sometimes wondered if the result were fair when you heard a lot of pals shouting out your name and applauding.

Just round the corner from the Odeon was a wee shopfront attached to a garage and they were Reliant Robin dealers, I always remember seeing pictures of these wee three wheeled cars. This was situated at the start of Almulree St.

I used to go to the shops at this end of Shettleston, the likes of A.F. Brown's for Matchbox motors. It was at the corner of Ardholm St. if I am correct. There was also a shop across the road that I used to buy a sixpenny balsa wood glider from, which I had loads of fun with. It had a slot that you could position the wings,(forward position for stunt flying, Backward position for long glides). They were well worth the money as they lasted quite a long time.

Maggie's Clootie Dumpling

THE PICTURES

I lived only a minutes' walk from the State picture house, which played a big part my early childhood. They would show two films, an A film and a second B film for three days, Mon.-Wed., and then change the film on a Thursday for the next three days. The State had a window that they wished the Shettleston Junior Football team good luck when they were in the final of The Scottish Junior Cup against Irvine Meadow, in 1959.

At the left-hand side of the State was Birrell's the sweetie shop. I used to go to the pictures by myself in those days when it was much safer to do so. I think because it was so close to the house, my parents felt it was ok, I mean, it was a sign of the times, you could leave a pram outside a shop safely, and there didn't seem the need to lock your door.

Sometimes I would be at the State twice in the one week, and I soon found out if you were accompanied by an adult, you got in for half price. So if I could get someone to take me in, I had more money to spend in Birrell's sweetie shop.

I don't know how many times I did this, but it was a lot. If my Ma and Da had found out they would have killed me. I carried on doing this into my teens, and my pals who were a couple years older than me, wanted to go and see their first X certificate film Dr. Crippen because they heard there was sex scenes in it, and I wanted to go with them.

Now I was just beginning to stretch, but I was still small, and looked young for my age. So I went to pictures with my pals and decided try my luck, I sort of mingled in amongst them, until I got to the kiosk to pay in, and it was the woman who was on most of the time, she took one look at me and said, "You want to make your mind up whether you're half price or an adult, and gave me my ticket.

I forgot to mention her wee sister was in my class at primary, she was the one who reported me for smashing a window with a tennis ball. So I don't know if it was because she knew me, that she let me in. I remember when the State showed The Ten Commandments, it ran for two weeks, and they were queuing every night.

I always loved the Art Deco style of the picture houses in those days, and the State Cinema was one of my favourites. I think it was the Evening Citizen that used to have a children's section near the back pages. It would be made up puzzles and games. One such puzzle was a maze which you had to find your way to the centre, and if you did you could win a prize.

So I thought I'll give it a try, only I started from the inside and worked my way-out tracing with my pen. I folded it up and put it in an envelope and posted it. They printed the names of the winners the next week, and I was amongst them. I can't remember if they sent the ticket that was the prize, or if you had it to get it at the Vogue cinema in Riddrie. That wasn't a problem for me as I could get the wee 30 bus across the road in Killin St. that went to just round the corner from it.

As I said I just loved the Art Deco and Art Nouveau period thing, and have done so all my life, especially in later years, when at one point I used to love the style of the ceramics and vibrant colours, practically anything from that era.

Art Nouveau Clock

TOM LAIRD

BUTCHER'S BOY

When I was about twelve and had left the primary school, the local butcher Wullie Henderson asked if I would like a part time job. At first it was Saturday mornings to deliver butcher meat to his customers. Now the transport was an old butchers bike with his name on it, complete with a basket at the front below the handlebars.

I don't know what height I was then, but my feet couldn't reach the ground. It was like a tank and felt as heavy as one. I tried that first day, mounting it by standing on a high kerb. The problem was trying to keep the thing upright when peddling and being able to do a quick dismount before the bike fell over. I told Wullie, the next

Saturday I would try and get a loan of my sisters bike.

Now the bike my sister had, which she hardly used had been built by her boyfriend George, who later would be her future husband. I wasn't allowed to use it, but I would sneak it out when she was at work. It was a cracking bike really light and fast, so this would be Ideal if I could borrow it. I asked George and Ellen at the same time and got their approval.

Although George was an enthusiastic cyclist, I now think he realised Ellen was never going to be one. I can't recall, but I managed to get a saddle bag by the time the following Saturday arrived, I was all set. Delivering the butcher meat was easy on this bike and I really enjoyed it. This was the start of me earning my own pocket money.

After a while Wullie asked me if I would like to work more hours. "I thought you only delivered on a Saturday "I said. "That's right, but I want you to come in after school on a Thursday and Friday to make sausages and clean the machines afterwards" he replied. "O.K." I enthusiastically replied.

So the following Thursday after school I reported to the shop, to be kitted out with a butchers apron that must have been made for a small person because it fitted me. I was given my first lesson on how to make Lorne sausages (square sliced) and how to clean everything that was used. One thing I enjoyed doing was scrubbing the butcher's block.

The process of making the sausages started with mincing the meat and adding the preservative and seasoning which was then pressed into a stainless-steel Lorne sausage tin, turned out, and then placed in the chill. Link sausages were different in the way they were produced.

The mix would be put into a cylindrical press that had an external tube at the bottom. When the pressure was put on the press by winding a handle, the meat would be pushed out of the tube that had sausage gut fed over it. The link sausage would then ooze out into the gut which was then twisted and tied at intervals to create individual links. These would then be chilled also.

I never got the chance to make Black Pudding. I don't know if this was something that was done earlier in the day before I arrived. The other thing that I made was Lard otherwise also known as dripping.

After the lean meat for the sausages was separated from the fat, before going into the mincer. The fat would then be put into a large cylindrical tub which was gas fired and would then melt it into lard. When there was enough, it would be fired up. After melting the fat, it would be left to cool down and set into lard.

Behind the Lard boiler was the window in the back shop, with bars on the outside, which made it feel a bit like a jail. To the left of the lard boiler was the sink, where the hot water would be almost boiling, scalding temperatures, all day.

When you looked inside the chill, it would be full sides of beef, that seemed enormous, hanging from large hooks, lamb would also be hanging up, and it had an assortment of sausages, black puddings, haggis and tripe. On a Saturday the frying pan would be on all day, with a selection of chops and sausages, constantly frying, but for some reason never burning.

One of the places I delivered to on a Saturday was St. Paul's Chapel House where the priests lived. The housekeeper's name if I remember right was Nellie. All of the deliveries I did had their name and price of their order written on the exterior brown paper wrapping.

She was a cheery woman, you always found her the same way, with a big smile and an infectious laugh. I could almost place her in Disney animation, with her red, rosy cheeks and thick glasses.

Sometimes when I went there when Canon Conlon was in the kitchen. In that environment he didn't seem the same stern man that I remember him being when he was taking mass. Maybe it was the Nellie effect. I could tell the priests were well fed going by the price of the meat bill. Nellie would always secretly slip me a tip, with a see you next week, goodbye.

The one regret I have now is when my Ma died, she was A staunch catholic and would never miss mass until later years when her health would not allow it. Her funeral which was on 8th December 1995, which normally a coffin would be placed at the centre front of the alter, but because it was a holiday of obligation (Immaculate Conception), her coffin was delegated to the left-hand side of the chapel. I suppose this is common practice, but for a wee woman who stuck by them all her years, she was no more than a number.

St. Pauls

Wullie was a bit of a gambler and liked a good drink. He was forever seen wearing his butcher's apron, and a felt fedora hat, smoking his pipe, going in and out of the bookies and then the Gartocher Bar next door to it. He had two daughters who were completely different to each other.

The one that used to help out on a Saturday with washing the implements, was a very quiet girl, I think she went to a private school. It was either that or they gave them a right posh uniform.

The other daughter that came in sometimes on a Thurs. or Fri. night was the exact opposite. It wasn't the first time she chased me around the butcher's block, but never caught me. The shop closed years later, I don't know if it was ill health or money problems, or if he retired.

WILLIAM HENDERSON
FAMILY BUTCHER
QUALITY MEATS

AMONG THE GRAVESTONES

My sister Sadie and myself at the Barras age about 12/13

LONG TROUSER SUIT

With my sister Ellen's wedding happening recently, in St. Pauls' It took place on Easter Monday 1962. My Da had bought me a long trouser suit for it. The reception was held in the old St. Pauls, which was now the chapel hall, opposite St. Pauls primary school. My Da, had bought all the drink for the reception from the Kirkhouse pub, who I think gave him a discounted price.

Everything went well, I had my first ever dance with my Ma, who was trying to teach me the St. Bernard's waltz without stepping on her toes. To round it all off I even got to sing The Young Ones on stage with the band, whose leader an accordion player, who was the brother of one of the primary school teachers, a Mrs McCormack.

This was when I started going to the Dennistoun Palais on Saturday afternoons after I had finished for the weekend with my work in the butchers. I went with my school pal Gerry and some others. It was my first long trouser suit. So that was me kitted out for the dancing.

This was when the twist was all the rage and Chubby Checker was given it laldy. The D.J.'s name I'm sure was Dean Jeffries. We were all pretty good at it. So much so that myself and another boy at school appeared on the stage at the now famous Wellshot Halls. In some playground fantasy. It was a production created by a teacher whose nickname was Bootsie. I don't know what her real name was. Another time I was in a singing concert held in the school gym, I just liked singing.

At this time is when the Beatles appeared on the scene, and I remember one of the girls that I knew, when we met her after she had been in the town and seen them, she was still hysterical and couldn't calm down.

I had now said goodbye to the butcher's job, and my pal Robert handed over his job as a paperboy to me, when he left school. It entailed, working every morning and evening for about 1.1/2 hours, but the pay was a lot more than at Wullie's butcher shop. A Sunday morning was the worst, the weight of those Sunday papers!.

Now I was able to buy clothes amongst other things. My sister Sadie's boyfriend Tommy whose mother ran a catalogue, and she would let me get clothes from it. They stayed in Balintore St. around the corner from my Da's auntie Maggie.

Tommy and his mother were very good to me. They would let me watch the wrestling on a Saturday afternoon, before we had a tv, and on a couple of occasions he would take me to see Celtic.

Tommy's dad used to coach in a boxing gym, and it must have been him that got Tommy, my sister Sadie and I, tickets for a boxing match in St Andrews Hall 4th May 1961 to see Dick McTaggart fight. At the end of the night he presented me with a programme with autographs of all the Scotland team from that night as well as Dick McTaggart's.

The following year we were back at the St. Andrews Hall, this time to see, Brenda Lee, Gene Vincent, **(Who would swing his leg over the microphone. Seemingly his leg was injured, and he had a steel sheath over it, so he made this part of his act.)** Also there were a few supporting acts in the show.

Tommy had a variety of different jobs, from being a train engine fireman to a bus conductor and a job in the Camp coffee essence factory, and sometimes bringing us the odd bottle of essence to our house. You always knew when Tommy was in the house, he used a lot of Old Spice after shave.

One of the times he was in our house, and I toppled the kitchen cabinet on top of myself because I had swung on the door. It gave him and my sister a pure fright, as they were sitting in the living room at the time. To their relief I was ok.

TOM LAIRD

I was always fascinated with gadgets and was amazed at the things that used to be advertised in American comics and bubble-gum wrappers, the likes of wristwatch tv's and radios. The only problem was you couldn't get them here.

When I was about 13 years old I bought a transistor radio when they first came out. I think it was from Coats record shop in Shettleston. I always have been into gadgets, and this must have been the start of it. I remember it cost me £13.00, to pay it up. It was a little red Perdio. They were not cheap when they first appeared in the shops. Coats also had a side entrance in Ardholm St, It had little booths to listen to the records that you were interested in.

Two or three years later when I was a vanboy with Welma Bakeries I purchased a lovely little Vesta Vixen transistor radio, which had a neat leather cover on it for £5.00 from Woolworths in Shawlands, so you can see how the price fell when they became more available.

AMONG THE GRAVESTONES

Perdio Transistor radio

Vesta Vixen Transistor radio

MY PALS

When I started the secondary school My pal was Gerry, who I remember being in a fight after school with another boy who thought he was the hardman of the class It was all over in a matter of minutes; he dumped the other guy in a dustbin at the back of the tenements that stood in front of the school. He stayed in a building in Shettleston Rd., just round the corner from Chester St.

We used to go to what we called record sessions. They were held in someone's house, and it really was an excuse to meet up play some records and maybe find a girlfriend. One such party that comes to mind, actually twice, was held in the living room of the funeral parlour that was situated on the corner of Chester St.. Angela whose house it was, said her mother didn't mind, even with the music getting played next door to where the coffins lay.

Myself and a couple of my classmates Jim and Wullie were selected to go on a course at the Inverclyde Sports Centre in Largs, that's where the Scotland football team used to train sometimes before a match. By this time I had started smoking which I shouldn't have, but a lot of my pals did.

If you were caught smoking here you would be sent home. One of the things we got was an orienteering exercise where you would be started off with a clue and given a map position, taught how to use the compass and off you went. We found the next clue and given a new heading to the next clue, and this would carry on until we reached our goal. We found that gradually we were heading up the hills.

As we got nearer to the top we were discovering all sorts of things, like a dead sheep in the mountain burn. The next thing we came across was a plane wreck, quite a fair-sized aeroplane It must have seated about twenty passengers. If I remember right we found a smaller plane, a Cessna type size.

Before we realised it a heavy mist had descended upon us. I began to think no wonder there is plane wrecks up here. We had wandered off course and we were lost.

But we had the original map coordinates from where we started. We would have to put our trust in what we were taught, as we had no other option. By now you couldn't see ten feet in front of you, and it was quite precarious as you couldn't see if there was any gullies. As we descended the mist began to thin out a bit, and eventually the sports centre came into view.

When I got back home, I went up to see my pals Davy and Robert and go out for a game of three and in. (If you scored three goals, it was your turn to become the goalie). I also had my first cigarette in two weeks, I should have stopped it there and then, but I didn't. I had been smoking for a few months. I stopped smoking when I turned 50. If I could go back again, I wouldn't have started.

AMONG THE GRAVESTONES

One place we used to frequent was The Shack in Springboig, which was basically what it was a shack. We went for the dancing and the group who was there regularly, Dean Ford and the Gaylords, who later went on to become The Marmalade. My favourite song of theirs is Reflections Of My Life. I particularly like the Dean Ford and Joe Tansin version.

Gerry who had a cousin called Billy, about a year later was starting a group, and told me he had an electric guitar for sale and would I be interested. He let me pay it up over four instalments of £5.00 with a free guitar lesson each time. I eagerly accepted the offer, only to find out I was rubbish, no coordination whatsoever.

I was really interested in singing, and the time when I was in Billy's house, they would be practising with an echo chamber, which I'd liked to have tried but never got the chance, maybe if I had just brass necked it and asked.

As I got older, I had a great set of pals, Davy Wallace, Robert Stott, Dougie Roy, Alec Mellis, Bobby Kerr, and Lester, from Provanhall, who I can't remember his surname. I was the only catholic amongst all my pals, and religion never came into it.

As a matter of fact in later years when we first started going into the town on a Sunday night for a drink, they would wait for me coming out of the chapel if I went to night mass. Anyway back to some of the things that we did when we were still at school.

Davy, Robert, and myself, would sometimes catch the new electric train from Shettleston train station to Helensburgh on a Saturday morning to go to the outdoor swimming pool. It was freezing even on the nicest of days. We would last only about 10 to 15 minutes in it. That reminds me the time as a toddler of about three, I dived into a paddling pond that was on the beach, and cracked my head. The water was only about 2ft deep. Something makes me think it was Helensburgh.

We used to hang about Davy's close on Shettleston Rd., it must have been a Friday or Saturday night, because that was usually when all the drunks came staggering along the road. We had this little plastic skeleton that was about 6 inches long, and someone came up with the idea of tying a length of heavy thread around its neck and throwing it over the street light wires or phone wires overhead.

Nobody even took into consideration if it was safe or not. So we managed to successfully throw it over. We hung about the close for some unsuspecting drunk to come along. I think it was the third one who came along that noticed it. A wee breeze had shifted it into his line of sight, "What the hell is that" he uttered, "Are ye alright son, you look as if you could do wi a wee bite to eat, and what are you doing hinging about here wi nae clathes on.

Well that was it we were rolling about with laughter, and someone lost their grip of the thread and it hit him right on the head. He heard the laughing, "Ya wee buggers" and started making a beeline for us and we all scarpered. That was the first and last time we tried that.

The first fish I ever caught properly; was a time when we were over on the island of Bute. We had hired a rowing boat round at Port Bannatyne, and my first cast into the water I hooked a fish. When I reeled it in I didn't know what type it was. "It's a Haddock, you can tell with the thumbprint on the side of its head" Davy enthusiastically remarked. We were only about 30 or 40 feet from the shore.

I don't think you would have any chance of that now, with all the trawlers fishing as close to the coast as they do now. A matter of fact, I think they have to go further out now as there is not much left inshore. I have never heard of anyone catching a haddock from the shoreline. I spent a lot of times with my pals at Rothesay over the years.

There was another incident that happened around from Davy's in Gatehouse St. when we were having a walk, and this boy bumped into Davy, before we knew it the two of them were fighting. Davy got the better of him with a couple of whacks to his jaw and it was all over. We didn't even know what it was all about.

It must have been about 15 minutes later when we were heading back to Davy's close that we saw what looked like a swarm of bees emerging from the St. Serf's church further along on the opposite side of the road. It wasn't bees it was a gang of guys, and they were heading our way. It was then we realised they were coming for us.

Davy and Robert were first into the close with me a good bit behind to only see the back of Robert disappear behind Davy's closed door. I had no option to run through the close and try and get over the wall into the muck. I was clambering up the wall and felt my legs getting tugged, but I managed to get over it to no avail. They came over behind me and caught me.

I was taken back to the church where I was put under the microscope, spotlight in my face, asking why we all attacked one of their own. These guys were in their 17's and 18's, and I said no mister we didn't touch him it was a fair fight, a square go, honest we never touched him.

They must have believed me because that is when they let me go. It turns out in later years, I was at a party in the house of the guy that was questioning me, although he never recognised me.

One of the things we would do on a Sunday was to go over the golf course past the first quarry, to go into Kings Motorcycles and look at all the scooters that they stocked. We were too young, but we always knew that is what we wanted to try when we left school and started working and reached 16 the age that we had to be to get a provisional licence.

That was years away, but it didn't stop us from dreaming. Approximately two years later we all had scooters.

AMONG THE GRAVESTONES

Our Dream

ON REFLECTION

I'm glad I was privileged to have been born when I was, for the parents I had, when there was a sense of values and trust. When an education meant you had to learn to count and spell, without all the reliance on digital devices. I suppose that's me the pot calling the kettle black.

What I mean is I can spell, I can count without a calculator, I think mental arithmetic is a thing of the past, but my writing is atrocious. I would not have been able to write this book without a computer, nor would you have been able to decipher any of my written text.

See What I Mean

AMONG THE GRAVESTONES

Kirkhouse 1903
Picture Courtesy of Kirkhouse Pub

Printed in Great Britain
by Amazon